The Duties and Responsibilities of
the Secretary of Education

David C. Ruffin

The Rosen Publishing Group's
PowerKids Press™
New York

To my mother, Frances, who was PTA president
of McElvy Elementary School

Published in 2005 by The Rosen Publishing Group, Inc.
29 East 21st Street, New York, NY 10010

First Edition

Editor: Frances E. Ruffin
Book Design: Albert B. Hanner
Photo Researcher: Sherri Liberman

Photo Credits: Cover (left), pp. 16 (top), 19 (left), 37 (bottom) © AP/Wide World Photo; cover (center), pp. 7 (left), 11, 28 (left) © Bettmann/Corbis; cover (right), p. 8 Courtesy: Jimmy Carter Library; cover (bottom), pp. 1, 4 © Steven Chenn/Corbis; p. 7 (right) © Topham/The Image Works; p. 12 (top) © Corbis; p. 12 (bottom) © Michael Mauney/Time Life Pictures/Getty Images; p. 15 (top) © Ed Quinn/Corbis; p. 15 (bottom) © AFP/Corbis; p. 16 (bottom) © Ed Kashi/Corbis; p. 19 (right) © Ellen Senisi/ The Image Works; p. 20 © Gabe Palmer/Corbis; p. 23 © Larry Williams/Corbis; p. 24 Courtesy of Howard University; p. 27 (left) © New York University Photo Bureau/Don Hamerman; p. 27 (right) © Mark Peterson/Corbis; p. 28 (clockwise from top left) © Bettmann/Corbis, © Corbis, (Bennett, Cavazos, Alexander) © Hulton/Archive/Getty Images; p. 28 (right) Courtesy of the U.S. Department of Education.

Library of Congress Cataloging-in-Publication Data

Ruffin, David C.
The duties and responsibilities of the Secretary of Education / David C. Ruffin.
     p. cm. — (Your government in action)
Includes bibliographical references and index.
ISBN 1-4042-2692-3 (lib. bdg.)
1. United States. Dept. of Education—Juvenile literature. 2. Education and state—United States—Juvenile literature. 3. Federal aid to education—United States—Juvenile literature. I. Title.

LB2807.R84 2005
379.73—dc22

2004000068

Manufactured in the United States of America

Contents

The Secretary of Education

The secretary of education is the head of the U.S. Department of Education. The present-day Department of Education, created in 1979, is one of the youngest **agencies** in the federal government. The secretary oversees programs that help the nearly 54 million children who attend the nation's more than 120,000 elementary and secondary schools. The Department of Education also oversees programs for students, teachers, and school administrators, or directors, at all levels of education, from preschool to university. The Department of Education is located in Washington, D.C. There are about 4,800 **employees** at the Department of Education who help the secretary to do his or her job. In recent years the department has spent more than $53 billion each year on programs to educate Americans.

◄ *The secretary of education works to make sure that students in America receive a quality education and that they learn the skills they need to be successful adults.*

A Changing Department

The U.S. Congress established the first Department of Education in 1867. It was part of the president's **cabinet**. The department's four workers collected facts about America's schools. In 1869, it was removed from the cabinet and became the Office of Education. During the mid-1900s, major social and **political** changes resulted in greater government spending on education. For example, the Union of Soviet Socialist Republics (U.S.S.R.) sent the first **satellite**, called *Sputnik I*, into space in 1957. America feared that it would fall behind the U.S.S.R. in science and **technology,** so the Office of Education spent more money on science education. Even more money was spent when President Lyndon B. Johnson began his War on Poverty in 1964, which called for better education for children from poor families. By 1965, the Office of Education had more than 2,000 workers.

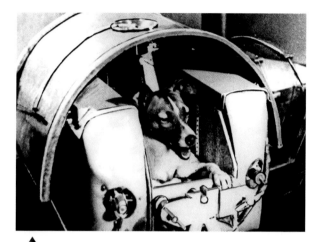

The U.S.S.R.'s launch of Sputnik I *set off what came to be known as the Space Race. Here Sputnik II is shown with its passenger, the dog Laika. This was the first satellite that carried a live passenger.*

Lyndon B. Johnson declared a war on poverty during his presidency. One of the programs he began as part of this effort was the Head Start Program. Head Start is a program for children from ages 3 to 5 who come from poor or disadvantaged backgrounds.

President Jimmy Carter signs the act that created the
new Department of Education in October 1979.

A New Department Is Created

Many people wanted the Office of Education to be an independent governmental agency. One group that wanted this was the National Education Association (NEA), a powerful organization to which many American teachers belonged. Connecticut senator Abraham Ribicoff also wanted an independent agency. He had been the secretary of the Department of Health, Education and Welfare (HEW) from 1961 to 1962. The Office of Education had been a part of HEW since 1953. He worked with the NEA and other educational groups to **convince** Congress to create the new Department of Education. In 1979, President Jimmy Carter signed the Department of Education Organization Act. The act took the many educational programs from HEW and created a separate Department of Education. The Department of Education began to operate in 1980.

9

The First Secretary

President Jimmy Carter appointed Shirley Hufstedler to be the first secretary of education. Before she became the secretary, she had been a lawyer and a judge. As secretary of education, she worked to bring all educational programs together to make the department operate smoothly. She also discovered some excellent educational programs in schools around the country. These programs were good examples for teachers and principals to use. Secretary Shirley Hufstedler believed that education was necessary to make the United States strong. She made many speeches to help citizens and political leaders understand the importance of education. Shirley Hufstedler formed a strong base on which later secretaries of the Department of Education could build.

Secretary Hufstedler said, "The role of the teacher remains the highest calling of a free people. To the teacher, America entrusts her most precious resource, her children, and asks that they be prepared . . . to [take part] in a democratic society."

Secretary of Education Terrel H. Bell (right) speaks with President Ronald Reagan (left) about the importance of the Department of Education's work.

Terrel H. Bell visits with a kindergarten class in Salt Lake City, Utah.

Convincing a President

In 1981, when Ronald Reagan took office as president of the United States, he appointed Terrel H. Bell of Lava Hot Springs, Idaho, to be the secretary of education. Terrel Bell knew a lot about education because he had been the commissioner of education at HEW before he became the secretary of education. President Reagan believed that, because the new Department of Education was a federal agency, it would **interfere** with schools operated by cities and states. He wanted Secretary Terrel Bell to **dismantle** the Department of Education. However, Secretary Bell convinced President Reagan that the department was useful and important. President Reagan changed his mind and allowed the Department of Education to continue, but he took some money away from educational programs.

New Goals

From 1988 to 1990, Dr. Lauro F. Cavazos served as secretary of education under presidents Ronald Reagan and George H. W. Bush. Cavazos had been president of Texas Tech University. He established a new set of **goals** for the nation's schools. Students were to be well-prepared to enter the first grade. The number of students **graduating** from high school was to increase. Cavazos wanted American students to lead the world in math and science. He also wanted all schools to be safe and drug free. In 1993, President Bill Clinton appointed South Carolinian governor Richard W. Riley as secretary of education. Secretary Riley **expanded** on the goals established by Cavazos and other secretaries of education. He wanted all students to succeed. He urged teachers to become better educated and parents to become more active in their children's education. His education plan became known as Goals 2000.

Secretary Riley (right), shown here with President Clinton (left), urged states to approve charter schools. More than 3,000 charter schools have opened since they were approved by state governments beginning in the 1990s.

A teacher instructs students at a charter school in Boston, Massachusetts. Charter schools are independent schools supported by federal money.

Secretary of
Education Rod
Paige (center)
wears a blanket
given to him by
the president of
the American
Indian Higher
Education
Consortium. Rod
Paige became the
seventh secretary
of education in
January 2001.

A young teacher
instructs a boy at
the Wellpinit
Elementary School
on the Spokane
Indian Reservation.

Elementary Education

The secretary of education oversees many programs created to help students succeed in school. The Office of Elementary and Secondary Education (OESE) supports states and their schools in helping students to do their best. The OESE provides money for schools in places that have less money for education, such as Indian **reservations**, small towns, and neighborhoods in big cities. One of OESE's programs is Title I, which is part of the Elementary and Secondary Education Act (ESEA). It gives funding to schools with a high number of students who come from poor families. Title I benefits more than 12.5 million students, mostly elementary students. Money from another program called Title II helps to make sure there is a teacher who is well qualified in every classroom.

The secretary of education advises the president on issues in education. He or she also works with Congress to pass important acts on education.

Finding Better Ways to Teach

The secretary of education makes sure that Americans can get a high-quality education. One way he or she does this is by making sure teachers have the **information** and support they need to succeed. The Institute of Education Sciences is the office of the Department of Education that focuses on research, or finding facts and information. The institute's research is available to schools to help improve how subjects are taught. Secretary of Education Rod Paige worked hard with the president to pass the No Child Left Behind Act of 2001. This important education act was signed into law by President George W. Bush in 2002. The goal of the act is to help every American child do better in school. It is important because many children in the fourth grade cannot keep up with their classmates in reading.

Secretary Rod Paige issued the Blueprint for Management Excellence to improve the management in the department and to help it be effective and trustworthy.

The Institute of Education Sciences helps teachers by finding new ways to teach that will help all children to learn.

Secretary Rod Paige discusses the No Child Left Behind Act of 2001. This act states that all children will receive the education and support they need to succeed in school.

In 1975, Congress ▶ passed a law known as Individuals with Disabilities Education Act (IDEA). As part of this act, all schools must make sure there is a way for children with physical disabilities to enter the school and attend classes with their friends.

Programs for All Kids

The secretary of education is in charge of programs that help all students, including those who need extra help. For example, some students who have come to the United States from other countries may enter school without being able to speak English. The secretary of education makes sure students who do not speak English have an opportunity to learn through special classes and textbooks that help them to read and write in English.

Some students have **physical** disabilities, such as blindness. Some students have other disabilities that make it hard for them to learn. The Department of Education pays for teachers and programs that help students with disabilities to learn. The Jacob K. Javits Gifted and Talented Students Education Program looks for new ways to discover and teach students with special abilities in math, writing, music, art, and other subjects.

The Nation's Report Card

Under Secretary Rod Paige's leadership, the Nation's Report Card improved. In 2003, the percentages of fourth graders performing at or above Basic, Proficient, and Advanced levels in mathematics were the highest they had been since 1990.

The secretary of education gets information on how schools are performing through the National Center for Education **Statistics**. This center collects information that can be useful to teachers, students, and parents. For example, it conducts the National Assessment of Educational Progress, which is also known as the Nation's Report Card. This report helps educators in all parts of the country compare how well the students in their district are doing. The center also reports on such facts as how many students graduate from high school, how many students are being home-schooled, the number of crimes that have occurred in schools, and other facts. Much of the funding for schools is based on how well a school measures up to other schools on these reports.

NCES
National Center for
Education Statistics

NAEP
Nation's
Report
Card

The Nation's Report Card
Trial Urban District **Reading** 2003
Assessment

New York City Public Schools
Grade 8
Public Schools

Snapshot Report

NCES 2004-453XN8

The National Assessment of Educational Progress (NAEP) assesses reading on a 0-500 point scale. In 2003, New York City Public Schools was one of nine urban districts that voluntarily participated in the NAEP reading assessment on a trial basis.

Overall Reading Results for New York City

- In 2003, the average scale score for eighth-grade students in New York City was 252. This was lower[1] than that of the nation's public schools (261).
- New York City's average score (252) in 2003 was not significantly different from that of public schools in large central cities[2] (249), and lower than that of New York (265).
- The percentage of students in New York City who performed at or above the NAEP *Proficient* level was 22 percent in 2003. The percentage of students in New York City who performed at or above the *Basic* level was 62 percent.

Student Percentage at NAEP Achievement Levels

New York City (Public)
2003: 38 | 40 | 20 | 2

Large central city (Public)
2003: 41 | 40 | 17 | 1

Nation (Public)
2003: 28* | 42 | 27* | 3

Percentage below Basic and at Basic — *Percentage at Proficient and Advanced*

■ below *Basic* □ *Basic* ▤ *Proficient* ■ *Advanced*

NOTE: The NAEP reading scale ranges from 0 to 500, with the achievement levels corresponding to the following points: Below *Basic*, 242 or lower; *Basic*, 243-280; *Proficient*, 281-322; *Advanced*, 323 or above.

Performance of NAEP Reporting Groups in New York City

Reporting groups	Percentage of students[3]	Average Score	Below *Basic*	*Basic*	*Proficient*	*Advanced*
Male	47 ↓	246 ↓	45 ↑	39	15 ↓	1
Female	53 ↑	257 ↓	32 ↑	41	24 ↓	3
White	13 ↓	270	21	38	36	6
Black	38 ↑	245	44	43	13	#
Hispanic	33 ↑	247	43	39	16	1
Asian/Pacific Islander	16 ↑	264	28	38	30	4
American Indian/Alaska Native	# ↓	—	—	—	—	—
Free/reduced-price school lunch						
Eligible	85 ↑	248	42	40	16	1
Not eligible	11 ↓	278	13	39	41	7

Average Score Gaps Between Selected Groups

- In 2003, male students in New York City had an average score that was lower than that of female students (11 points). This performance gap was not significantly different from that of the Nation (11 points).
- In 2003, White students had an average score that was higher than that of Black students (25 points). This performance gap was not significantly different from that of the Nation (27 points).
- In 2003, White students had an average score that was higher than that of Hispanic students (23 points). This performance gap was not significantly different from that of the Nation (27 points).
- In 2003, students who were not eligible for free/reduced-price school lunch had an average score that was higher than that of students who were eligible (30 points). This performance gap was not significantly different from that of the Nation (25 points).

Reading Scale Scores at Selected Percentiles

Scale Score Distribution

	25th Percentile	50th Percentile	75th Percentile
New York City	229 ↓	254 ↓	277 ↓
Large central city (Public)	226 ↓	251 ↓	274 ↓
Nation (Public)	240	264	286

An examination of scores at different percentiles on the 0–500 NAEP reading scale at each grade indicates how well students at lower, middle, and higher levels of the distribution performed. For example, the data above show that 75 percent of students in public schools nationally scored below 286, and 75 percent of students in New York City scored below 277.

The estimate rounds to zero. — Reporting standards not met; sample size insufficient to permit a reliable estimate.
* Significantly different from New York City. ↑ Significantly higher than, ↓ lower than appropriate subgroup in the nation (public).
[1] Comparisons (higher/lower/not different) are based on statistical tests. The .05 level was used for testing statistical significance. Performance comparisons may be affected by differences in exclusion rates for students with disabilities and limited-English-proficient students in the NAEP samples and changes in sample sizes. NAEP sample sizes have increased since 2002 compared to previous years, resulting in smaller detectable differences than in previous assessments.
[2] "Large central city" includes nationally representative public schools located in large central cities within metropolitan statistical areas as defined by the federal Office of Management and Budget. It is not synonymous with "inner city."
[3] For comparison, minority students comprised 77 percent of students in large central city public schools and 39 percent in public schools nationally. Also, students eligible for free/reduced-price school lunch comprised 60 percent of students in large central city public schools and 36 percent in public schools nationally.
NOTE: Detail may not sum to totals because of rounding, and because the "Information not available" category for Free/reduced-price lunch is not displayed. Statistical comparisons are calculated on the basis of unrounded scale scores or percentages.
SOURCE: U.S. Department of Education, Institute of Education Sciences, National Center for Education Statistics, National Assessment of Educational Progress (NAEP), 2003 Trial Urban District Reading Assessment.

▲

States use tests to tell them how students are doing in school.

◀ *The Nation's Report Card tells the secretary of education how American students are performing in various subjects. The report is very important because a lot of funding depends on its findings.*

OPE gives money to Historically Black Colleges and Universities, such as Howard University in Washington, D.C. Many of these schools were started in the late 1800s, when black students were not allowed to attend other colleges and universities. Today students of any race can go to school. Here students graduate from Howard University.

College and Beyond

The secretary of education is in charge of the Office of Postsecondary Education (OPE). The OPE oversees more than 40 programs and provides millions of dollars to help colleges and universities. It works to make sure that all students can get an excellent education. Some of the OPE's money goes to supporting students who may not have access to a good education otherwise. The OPE supports schools with a large number of these kinds of students by paying for new buildings, computers, and equipment. The office supports Historically Black Colleges and Universities. The OPE also offers programs that allow American students to study in other countries. One such program is the Fulbright-Hays grant program. It is awarded to individuals or groups who are interested in studying the languages, cultures, and arts of **foreign** countries.

The Department of Education's Office of Federal Student Aid (FSA) provides federal aid to college students through scholarships and loans.

Protecting Students' Rights

It is the secretary of education's job to make sure that all Americans receive an education. Until 1954, many African American students were not allowed to go to school with white students. In 1954, in the case *Brown v. Board of Education*, the Supreme Court ruled that racial **discrimination** in schools was illegal. The Department of Education's Office of Civil Rights was created to stop discrimination in schools and to make sure that all students have access to an excellent education. The Education **Amendments** of 1972 required schools to offer girls and boys an equal chance to play school sports. It also **enforced** laws protecting students with disabilities. The secretary of education works to make sure that students are not treated unfairly because of their race, gender, or disability. He or she works to make sure that America's educational system provides young people with the tools that will help them to shape America's future.

The secretary of education's job begins with young children. Every student must be provided with the right start in learning to read, write, and interact with others. These are important skills they will need throughout their lives.

Today students of all races can enjoy the benefits of a college education.

Secretaries of Education from 1979 to 2005

Shirley M. Hufstedler, 1979–1981

Terrel H. Bell, 1981–1985

William Bennett, 1985–1988

Lauro F. Cavazos, 1988–1990

Lamar Alexander, 1991–1993

Richard W. Riley, 1993–2001

Rod Paige, 2001–2005

Shirley M. Hufstedler
1979–1981

Rod Paige
2001–2005

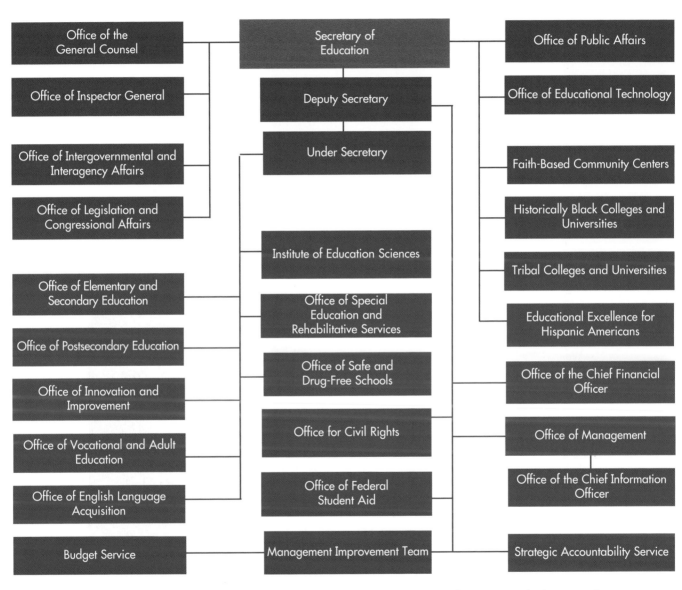

Office of the General Counsel	Secretary of Education	Office of Public Affairs
Office of Inspector General	Deputy Secretary	Office of Educational Technology
Office of Intergovernmental and Interagency Affairs	Under Secretary	Faith-Based Community Centers
Office of Legislation and Congressional Affairs		Historically Black Colleges and Universities
	Institute of Education Sciences	Tribal Colleges and Universities
Office of Elementary and Secondary Education	Office of Special Education and Rehabilitative Services	Educational Excellence for Hispanic Americans
Office of Postsecondary Education	Office of Safe and Drug-Free Schools	Office of the Chief Financial Officer
Office of Innovation and Improvement	Office for Civil Rights	Office of Management
Office of Vocational and Adult Education	Office of Federal Student Aid	Office of the Chief Information Officer
Office of English Language Acquisition		
Budget Service	Management Improvement Team	Strategic Accountability Service

The secretary of education has many duties and responsibilities. The 4,800 people who help the secretary work in the agencies of the Department of Education that are outlined in this chart.

29

Timeline

1867	The Department of Education Act establishes the first U.S. Department of Education.
1869	The Department of Education is removed from the president's cabinet and becomes an office.
1917	The Smith-Hughes Act provides money to states for vocational education, or job education programs.
1946	Harry S. Truman signs a bill to start the National School Lunch Program, which provides low-cost or free school lunches.
1958	The National Defense Education Act provides assistance to schools to strengthen instruction in science, math, and foreign languages.
1964	Congress enables the Department of Education to provide money and other help to schools and teachers at schools where black children and white children attend together for the first time.
1972	The Title IX Amendment enables girls to have the same opportunities as boys to participate in school-sponsored sports programs.
1994	An act is passed to prepare young people for their first jobs and for continuing education through School-to-Work programs.
1998	The Charter School Expansion Act provides government money to schools that are not part of the public school system.
2002	The No Child Left Behind Act of 2001 is signed into law.

Glossary

agencies (AY-jen-seez) Special departments of the government.

amendments (uh-MEND-ments) Additions or changes to the Constitution.

cabinet (KAB-nit) A group of people who act as advisers to important government officials.

convince (kun-VINTS) To make a person believe something.

discrimination (dis-krih-mih-NAY-shun) Treating a person badly or unfairly just because he or she is different.

dismantle (dis-MAN-tul) To take something apart piece by piece.

employees (im-ploy-EEZ) People who are paid to work.

enforced (en-FORSD) To have put or kept in force.

expanded (ek-SPAND-ed) To have spread out, or to have grown larger.

goals (GOHLZ) Things that a person wants and tries to get or become.

graduating (GRAH-joo-wayt-ing) Finishing a course of school.

information (in-fer-MAY-shun) Knowledge or facts.

interfere (in-ter-FEER) To disturb or prevent something.

physical (FIH-zih-kul) Having to do with the body.

political (puh-LIH-tih-kul) Having to do with the work of government or public affairs.

reservations (reh-zer-VAY-shunz) Areas of land set aside by the government for Native Americans to live on.

satellite (SA-tih-lyt) A machine in space that circles Earth and is used to track weather.

statistics (stuh-TIS-tiks) Facts in the form of numbers.

technology (tek-NAH-luh-jee) Industry that deals with electronics and computers.

Index

Web Sites

Due to the changing nature of Internet links, PowerKids Press has developed an online list of Web sites related to the subject of this book. This site is updated regularly. Please use this link to access the list:
www.powerkidslinks.com/yga/drse/